POETRY NOW LONDON & HOME COUNTIES 2003

Edited by

Katie Coles

First published in Great Britain in 2002 by
POETRY NOW
Remus House,
Coltsfoot Drive,
Peterborough, PE2 9JX
Telephone (01733) 898101
Fax (01733) 313524

HB ISBN 0 75434 385 5
SB ISBN 0 75434 386 3

FOREWORD

Although we are a nation of poets we are accused of not reading poetry, or buying poetry books. After many years of listening to the incessant gripes of poetry publishers, I can only assume that the books they publish, in general, are books that most people do not want to read.

Poetry should not be obscure, introverted, and as cryptic as a crossword puzzle: it is the poet's duty to reach out and embrace the world.

The world owes the poet nothing and we should not be expected to dig and delve into a rambling discourse searching for some inner meaning.

The reason we write poetry (and almost all of us do) is because we want to communicate: an ideal; an idea; or a specific feeling. Poetry is as essential in communication, as a letter; a radio; a telephone, and the main criterion for selecting the poems in this anthology is very simple: they communicate.

CONTENTS

PLAYING THE NUMBERS GAME

Some numbers express a void
with no relation one to the other,
yet like fish in ice, we can be trapped

seeing things in places never guessed
where images do not conform to human kind
and where being blind to our experiences

we have no chance to arrive at infinity
and smell the flowers of success
or engage with the sun,

to see the possibility of the expansion
of our mind from the mundane
and from the abstract to the specific.

The logic of the number sequence
is a trap set by our mind
which seeks all conformity and balance.

Yet ranging through the stars
no balance, no conformity is found
the very nature of surprise

defeats our tidy patterns
locked through logic
to even up the odds.

No rule of physics thus applied
can prepare us for surprise
and that itself is tragic.

Graham K A Walker

WOKINGHAM

Wokingham's a mixture of the old and new,
But traditional values still shine through.
Georgian and Tudor styles happily blend,
With new buildings showing the latest trend.
The splendid new library's modern and bright,
The council building's a planner's delight.
I once had a house in the centre of town
With a lovely old wall, now sadly pulled down.
Developers came, and altered the place
A fine large superstore now fills the space.
Most of the people who live here I find
Are very polite and exceedingly kind.
Wokingham's a town with a rural heart,
Where parks, trees and gardens all play their part.
Attractive churches, interesting to view,
Stand waiting to help the spiritual you.
There are excellent clubs which you will find
Help to stimulate both body and mind.
You can, at the end of a busy day
Visit the theatre, and see a good play.
There are numerous places where you can dine
And enjoy tasty food with a bottle of wine.
Good friendships and beer can be easily found
In the many inns, that are dotted around.
So as you can see, when all's said and done
Living in Wokingham's pleasant and fun.

Margaret Nixon

BIRDSONG ECHOES

An icy wind stirs powdered snow
Bare branches of trees reach for the sky
Rivers and streams have ceased to flow
And birdsong echoes as I walk by

In summer plentiful wildlife leaps
To hide in every bush and hedge
But now in winter the countryside sleeps
And ghostly birdsong echoes out instead

As snow lies thick upon the ground
Unmarked by the footprints of man or beast
The silence spreads all around
And birdsong echoes to the east

The song that leads me on and on
Comes from no source that I can see
But brightens up the icy dawn
These echoes of summer that are sung to me

R H Ashley

Beauty My Love

Beauty, my love, is but as the morning dew,
its short bloom upon the garden green,
sparkles for a time until the sun breaks through
and then to vanish, as if it had never been.
Beauty is a flower whose frail flesh
wrinkles will devour, and time defaces
hour by hour, in the erosion of our days.
Soon does it fade that makes the fairest flourish,
and short be the vanity of the virgin rose,
her blush that you so lovingly do nourish
yet which in time you must be forced to lose,
for too soon comes age, your strength abuse
and weighted by the burden of your years
will bend your dotage, homeward to the Earth,
now time has made a permit for your fears
that holds the Earth in ever changing state;
all our entries, in his book of fate
are written sure, and have their certain date
to close - as for beggar, as for king - the story of our days
when clothed in beauty, from dust shall fly
to lands of rapture, where nature's laws do not apply.
For Heaven is our heritage, Earth but a player's stage.

But I will tell you no more, this has been so often told,
Yet still remains our greatest fear, the fear of getting old.

H Parry

WHAT IS LOVE?

Love is a powerful fantasy,
At first all joy and delight,
Arriving unasked but welcome
Does God alone have the secret?

Change takes over our lives,
When love and desire in us stir.
Love knows no pity or mercy.
Excitement only two can share.

Lovers ignore every obstacle,
Nothing will keep them apart,
They cling even closer together,
Dreams entwine them heart to heart.

Stories need beautiful settings,
Handsome and expensive places,
But love treats rich and poor alike,
It's more than just flowers and graces.

Love may be shy and retiring,
But sometimes it's blinding attraction.
Caring and kindly, but selfish,
It's a maze of contrasting emotion.

So is love a form of madness?
Illusions can mislead the mind.
Love may too soon take its leave,
So we learn how to be worldly wise.

Sheila Rowland

New Beginnings

The sun is rising on another day,
A day that never dawned before,
A heavenly spectrum foreordained
By Holy will, but never ever seen before
In this same pattern, with our human eyes.
A day unique, unprecedented,
And all unknown, as is our destiny.

I look upon a newborn baby's face -
A child ne'er cradled in my arms before.
She is unique, beloved and beautiful,
With large dark eyes and lips unparalleled
In shape and form.
The wonder of creation! - How does the Lord of all
Fashion such infinite diversity
Of face and feature
In the teeming millions of mankind?

New dawn; new life
Unfolding like a flower.
What will the future hold, for
Emily Charlotte, three days old?

Jean Jackson

I Need You . . .

I need you to hold me
Hold me now.
Strength against silkiness
Sweat on my brow.

I need you to kiss me
Kiss me, but slow -
Passion through habit
Can still swell and grow.

I need you to love me
Love me, please
Then the pain of our parting
May ease.

Lilian Perriman

Stepping Stones

(Dedicated to Gina, John, Abbie and Mollie)

Look at the moon when the miles between us are vast
For you will sense my presence in the shadows that are cast,
Gaze towards the sunrise when our parting weighs on you,
For it will soothe your pining heart with cool, crack of dawn dew.
Stroll through summer meadows when your thoughts reflect on home
For the fresh scents that embrace you will show, you are not alone,
Search beyond the twilight if your expectations should
founder and fade,
Find the courage to cross life's stepping stones and barriers
you have made,
Heed whispers of encouragement that drift on the ebbing tide,
Walk tall, and I will walk with you, forever by your side,
Most of all look towards the heavens and multiply by ten
the stars above,
Then you will know how much we have to share as kindred love.

Sandra Edwards

Afternoon Discovery

Locked securely
coloured red
on the rails
'Hardrock' name
where pigeons fed
no wheels
in Camberwell
nor front forks
by a busy lane
the saddle gone
near Denmark Place
no handlebar
to cycle frame
pavement settled
without pedals
and missing
driving chain.

Reg C H Baggs

CRAIG

Lose me in sleep
for whilst I am there I can be away from the mind
that misses him so much.
Lose me in sleep
so that I'm not aware in my conscious mind that he's not next to me
that I can't feel him close to touch.
Lose me in sleep
so that the time when I'm near to him grows closer
and the void doesn't seem so vast.
Lose me in sleep
And when I awake let me see his eyes
at last.

Julie White

Walking With Earthquakes

Life is like that - a sort of walk
With earthquakes; calamities that stalk
Our route, and trip us up,
To drain away the well-charged cup
And invalidate our best intent.
But, bear in mind, when human attributes are spent
There is one who looks upon us all with favour,
Our one, our own, and indefatigable Saviour
Who lived and died for our sakes,
But rose again, unvanquished, from a grave of shame,
That we might walk with earthquakes
And glorify his Name.

Nigel Chisholm

My Father's Illusions

My father went to sleep during Compline
on a dull evening after Middlemass.
His brain was mashed livid with memories,
an athlete's mind in a crippled casing

There, father's woken at heathen Matins:
force-fed breakfast of kidneys, toast, coffee
with Calvados, marmalade and salt herring.
Another perfect day in Death's Valley
when the rime has melted into dug earth.
Afterwards the taxi to the bookies,
the music of unconscionable corks pulled
from a vintage symphony of bottles
for the celebration of also-rans.
The party includes the woman who will
one day be my mother. She smiles at him,
a genie in an eternal flagon,
and in that way she smiles at everyone.
He anticipates the familiar,
gnawing at the coming disappointment.
Perhaps that's poignant; for him it's torture
(he remembers it from when he still breathed).
The dead-cart won't call - but it approaches.
The day's perfect, a fritillary lands
on his sleeve, the comic death-head leering.

From life I'm remembering a dead man
comparing a pointless seamless memory
with its shadow and a broken promise.
What a day my father's death might have been.
He should have stolen another man's day.
I think of a wayward decision

- made in God's hearing, me the first witness -
never to change what had been, nor regret.
My father was a fool, tricked by cheap bibles,
our Hell is a repetitive Heaven.

John Halladay

POETRY

Writing poetry can be such a joy
It's like having a secret toy
Only 'You' control the words
Your very own thoughts
About the things you love,
Your need to write about them
The sunshine, the sunsets
The music you store inside you
The beauty all around
The sad things that happen
But this is life,
And poetry can convey so much
Words stored inside your head
Bursting to be said
You pick up your pen
And write about them
And this to me
Is poetry.

J Nicoll

HEAD BUTTON

I'm the top most button on the baby's cardie, out of ladybirds one,
two, three
and being the one at the top, I am bound to be leader you see.
Now you'd think that this would be easy, to be at the front of the queue
to tell all the other buttons, when to do up and undo.
To give the signal when to start, to advise on the best kind of tension
to burst at the first sign of trouble, or get the best of attention.
To be a kind of badge, for brave service, like a medal on a soldier's vest
or a beacon that shines up nobly right at the top of the chest.
But being top ladybird button is not all it's cracked up to be,
for waiting under the baby's chin, I should get an extra fee.
Feeding times are the worst bit, for baby is as keen as mustard
although there is plenty for everyone, I get most of the custard.
I don't mind the chocolate pudding, or apricot puree each day
but second-hand gravy and veggies, kind of take your breath away.
I don't know what it is about chicken, beef casserole or rice
but more often than not when the babe has a lot I see it again at
least twice.
Yes I get fed much more than the others, I know that I'm
never forgotten
but sometimes I feel just once in a while, I'd swap places with the one
at the bottom.

David Heffer

The Challenge To Nature

God and nature are related,
Nature responds where God dictated.
Humans attempt to intervene, with ideas
Some of which are so obscene,
They do not deserve even a thought.
But these humans challenge nature.
So their ideas are bought. - Nature is aghast.
Humanity handling the creation of life!
Children should be born through love,
With a blessing from above.
Not ejected, preserved, injected, inspected -
Then expected to be perfect, as nature would have them delivered.
Sometimes - God will pause -
Maybe relax for a worthy cause!
Nature in a different form, humans cannot hope to manage -
Nor would wish to.
Create a storm, to cause destruction with a powerful hand
To flood the land. God has the power to strike at any hour.
Cause devastation, expiration - termination -
Where, when, and of what He chooses.
In a challenge, humanity loses!

Doris L Huff

Wolf

As night creeps in, the full moon rises
Distantly heard is the howling of wolves.
Lying in the darkness the time has come.
The metamorphosis has just begun.
I feel myself changing, the tingling starts,
The smell of the world is opening up.
From human to wolf, the transition is done.
A fight for survival now a monster become.
As I stalk through the forest, looking for prey,
The sun starts to rise, the dawn of the day.
Frightened and lonely, I wander alone.
Desperate to find a pack of my own.
Lurking around, my nose to the ground
Smelling and listening for the tiniest sound.
My eye catches food the hunger sinks in
Cunningly watching as it walks in my den.
I pause, then lunge, my fangs sinking deep
Tearing and tasting the meat that's so sweet.
The sun has arisen; it's time to go back
The metamorphosis begins again.

Bhavna Dhokia

BLESSED COUNTRY

I close my eyes, the soft wind touches my cheeks,
From the distance children's voices call,
I hear the gentle gurgle of the river
And the cascading waterfall.

So many, many years I have been away
From this beloved land of my birth,
Now once again I am back home again
My feet firmly planted
On my country's blessed earth.

I look above to see the weeping willow's,
Foliage in sweet abundance grow,
The moorhen and the singing of the skylark
Sun shining and the river's gentle flow.

Far away in this world I have wandered
Across the mighty rivers of foreign lands,
Over the highest mountains
And the beaches' golden sands.

Never more will I wander
For I know wherever I may roam
There is nowhere in this whole wide world
That I could call my Heaven,
This is my beloved country, my home.

Gladys Bree

Actions

our every action
reactions to our past
will new resolve
lessen last?

our conduct changes
shifts lists
twists
turned
as past experience
spurned unlearned!

spent vanished
memory banished
bygones forgotten
so expensively begotten!

yesterday's yearnings
in dreams we sigh
languish lamely
as ambitions
dwindle die!

values veer vacillate
manners modify mutate
standards sink subside
deflate
fading fast!

all actions our
reactions to the past!

Brian Strand

THE LOST GALLEON

The waves were like a sandstorm, the froth burning alight.
The current was like a tornado so the fishes had to fight.
The mist was like a steam train, passing through the air
And out of it came the bow, closer, closer,
And there was the lost galleon, giving a long wide stare.

A storm blew up, the thunder roared, the lightning gave a flash.
The crew gazed up at the evil sky, but the mast then gave a crash.
The hero drew his weapons, the ship robber made a sound.
The hero chased, his pistols drawn, faster, faster,
And then suddenly the ship robber tripped and tumbled to the ground.

So the ship robber stopped running, they had a hand fight on a ledge.
They were fighting right on the ship's front, but they both
fell off the edge.
The hero and the robber were alive no more,
But the lost galleon went further, further, further.
The lost galleon went further, looking for the shore.

Mark Chapman (9)

My Buckinghamshire

On reaching Buckinghamshire the traveller will find
The countryside is beautiful and the people are kind
Whichever way they turn, their eyes open wide
On a sparkling wonder that the hills provide
Aylesbury and Buckingham and Milton Keynes too
Others I could mention all wait in a queue
The winding lanes, the shady trees
The broad green fields, the busy bees
The heightened sense of rural pride
Where gardens blossom like a glowing bride
In houseproud dwellings on everyone's wall
Trailing baskets of blooms invite you to call
Towns and villages in architectural delight
Flourish historically in their awesome might
Pubs and hotels promise gourmet pleasure
To welcome the hungry and weary at leisure
I could go on forever in unstinting praise
For this proud home of beauty, this land of amaze

Royston E Herbert

SPRING IS HERE

Now winter is over and spring is here
Open your eyes and use your ears
Some flowers are in bloom with fragrance sweet
Listen to the birds as they try and compete
They have so much to say now it is spring
You might even hear a nightingale sing
Or a woodpecker as it pecks at a tree
Their colours blend in so they're quite hard to see
Some trees are already a rich leafy green
While others are still 'sleeping', not a leaf to be seen
It is only April, we've a long way to go
Instead of April showers we might get snow
There's so much to see, it's changing every day
Nature is incredible, I say thank you when I pray

Yvonne King

How Many Times

How many times does a coward die?
How many teardrops make a sigh?
How many times can one heart break
At the hands of those who only take?

How many times can the wheels of fate
Show you the prize then bid you wait?
How much longer must young men die
At the whim of some politician's lie?

How many years does it take to learn
When the good luck comes that it's not your turn?

How many years still lie ahead,
Of lonely nights in a single bed?

How many times can you bounce right back
To suffer again on the self same rack?
What do you get for being meek?
A hearty slap on the other cheek.

Naida Davies

MOVING ON

This is my time,
I've lived your time,
Found a new rhyme.
Time to move,
Time to groove.
Time to search a new life,
Turn my back on this strife.

Searching and spinning,
Looking and waiting,
This is me, moving on,
Old life is gone.

What's on offer?
Something new?
Something for the few?
Time for a life review.
Think you know me?
Looking cool I see,
Happy are we?

Searching and spinning,
Looking and waiting,
This is me,
Moving on,
Old life is gone.

This is me, living a new life,
Say goodbye to old life.
This is me, moving on.
Why not come with me?
This journey's free.
You know you can,
I could be your man.

Searching and spinning,
Looking and waiting,
This is me, moving on,
Old life is gone,
Old life is gone,

I'm moving on.

Simon Icke

LOST FOR WORDS

I am trying to write a poem.
'Word thoughts' won't enter my head.
My life is in the doldrums
I might as well go to bed.
Dark clouds now fill the sky,
All I want to do is cry.
Tomorrow will a glimmer of light break through
To let a smile once more come into view?
We have to go on.
We need to be strong.
My happy 'word thoughts' I need to find,
For now I fear they have left me behind.

Patricia M Farbrother

HOMEWARD BOUND

Stormy seas may surround us,
And sharks may circle below.
Storm clouds swirl above us,
And we may be tossed and blown.

But we are crew in the master's ship,
And He is at our helm,
And He will safely guide us
To His heavenly harbour's realm.

So take courage and be sturdy,
Though we may be tossed around.
For God knows the course we've chartered
And He will lead us home.

And just as suddenly the storm will end.
The grey clouds shall disappear.
The sun shall kiss the crystal seas
And we will feel Him near.

Doves shall circle above us,
And dolphins shall leap in joy.
Ships' horns will fill the air in welcome
As our sails point us finally home.

S Charleston

MEMORIES

Memories like fading leaves, gather in the heart.
We remember loved ones that are now apart.
Through you, I am enriched in countless ways,
And will always remember those precious days.
Oh! Memory, what a blessed thing.
What a golden benediction you seem to bring.

Marion Edwards

Bacchanalia At Baby-Lon-Don!

The Red Ken's-and mine-estate, with crumbling walls,
Which is full of crannies, crevices and nasty holes,
Violently penetrated by the hemp's stink and smoke,
All mixed with a nauseating smell of beer and Coke!

Wild sex-orgies, noise, drinking; the cracking bones,
Sweaty bodies jumping, screaming; hitting bare stones!
All tongues, races, mixed; just like the Old Babylon.
Yet it isn't old; rather modern and new Baby-Lon-Don!

There without respect, people pollute the earth and sky,
And ask, 'But why do we need gods, when we too can fly?'
Tower of Babylon 'destroyed by gods', it must be a lie!
Yet in building even taller towers of Babylondon we vie.

Then the men make war, and a river of innocent blood flows,
While the 'angels of war' exchange countless martial blows.
And just for yellow or 'black gold' many people get killed,
So, 'Prince of Darkness' triumphs again on the battlefield!

But, to stop war, God of life, love and light; a wise Lord,
Sent the loving peace, with a good, wise and *truthful* word,
Which said, 'O, never shall I change my good and wise mind',
So, 'Be the priest eternal of righteous Melchizedek's kind'!

And 'Be just judge-dan-to all those who are living in sin'.
Then, 'Be leader in the last battle, which light must win'
So, good and wise Lord will always lead 'thy right hand',
In crushing all the wicked rulers of every 'sinful land'.

Geo Zoriastro

Picture This

It was good then, our life
It was so good
I wish I had a picture,
A picture of you
To show the world
So they could see how good it was

We were floating through the soundscape
Playing hopscotch on stars
Did we eat?
Did we drink?
Were we touched by
The granite life at all?

I was curled up in the nest of you
Feeling vaporised, weightless and high.
So, why did the cutters come,
Come to cut us down?
I wish I had a picture of us
To show the world
How good it was, don't you?

Chris Wright

FREEDOM

Freedom is within us,
So carry no burdens,
No yoke of addictions,
No secrets or vices.
Bathe in enlightenment,
Embracing integrity,
Bestowing compassion,
Discovering freedom.
Loving and loved,
From now to eternity.

Christine Clark

CHILDREN!

Even well before they're born
They can really make you sick,
And then the weight just piles on
You're no longer like a stick!
Nine months later there's not much space
For junior to wriggle,
It's time to join the big wide world,
Now this bit is a giggle . . . !
Pushing and shoving, gas and air
And so much more fun too,
Till the baby pops out, either way
Now what do you do?
Washing, feeding, changing
Just repeat these three for years
The only thing that changes
Are the growing little dears!
Teething, terrible twos (and threes!)
And all the potty fun
Nursery gives the mums a rest,
Or a chance to get chores done!
And then it's off to infant school
The years have really flown
Our little people aren't so small
Too quickly they have grown.
The stroppy teenage years await
With backchat and the 'hump'
How often do we think back
To that growing little bump?
But even all the hard work
And no money and no sleep,
Children bring a lot of fun
(As well as make you weep!)

Tears of laughter, pride and anger
Tears of pain and tears of joy
But there's nothing like a parent's love
For their special girl or boy.

Lorna D Savill

NW3

Obese old pigeons hang about
and watch a jaundiced sun go down;
a dead balloon, stuck in a dying tree -
detritus from the Jubilee -
completes the evening for me.
Why stay in this polluted town?

Well . . . 200 yards away
there's the Café Paradiso,
a low-life place to which I go
almost every other day,
where the waitresses present me
with a glass of *vino*, free!

And there's Druscilla, in the Deli,
who kindly sets aside for me
delicious walnut bread and turkey.
(From the front, Druscilla's comely,
but snide observers claim to find
that she's a little plump behind!)

Then there's my near neighbour, Claire.
I should perhaps confess that she
is *très petite* and apt to wear
a perfume that seduces me.
(If not for Claire I couldn't bear
to dwell in this vicinity!)

Frank Dunnill

OLD NORTH: *WEST YORKSHIRE*

Sunsets are tattered vermilion,
Winter stars diamond pins
Piercing Pennine skies.
Nights swing to icy dawns,
Snow hushing the lanes,
Muffling stone angles . . .

Rough moor-men hewed
The standing stones,
Temples to gods of Elmet.
Came the Brigantes, Vikings,
Anglians. Delvers of millstone grit
And Ashlar; beetle-browed weavers
Inheriting old words:
'Thoil' and 'throng' and 'Sithee'!

From stone farmhouses
In clay-clogged fields
Towns grew like wildfire
In the white noise of looms.

These old shadows will fall forward
When Old North returns,
As we shall,
To moor and night and wind.

June Benn

A K(NIGHT) IN THE OFFICE

On the 122nd high-rise floor
No one ever looks at this door
'Why doesn't anyone ever knock?'
Sighed worried man in heavy shock

Looking out into the night
He saw nothing that gave delight
Empty car parks, lots of rain
Devoid of people, a running drain

What to do - glanced at the clock
No alternative but to lock -
The door - leading to the place
That had made him squirm in disgrace

Consider the crime that he has done
'Twas only intended in good fun
He's locked the door on the meter man
Ignored his cries - 'Bang, bang, bang'

Hours later, nothing was heard
The sound of silence - really absurd
An open door - no one there
Had the meter man crashed down the stair?

The stair was clear - nobody at all
No one lying against the wall
A deepening mystery - no sign of him
Not even a trace of human skin

'Meter man - Where are you?'
Shrilled his voice - not clear or true
A ghastly moan in reply
Voiced 'MM' from the sky.

A silent whistle - with ghostly breath
Sent out all the air from his chest
Scared to death - no longer aloof
He staggered to top of high-rise roof

'Tickle, tickle' under his chin
A bony finger followed him
This was too much - to his death he flew
Without a sound or hullabaloo!

Ray Boyce

Sandals And Boots

Down in Oxleas Wood the centurion stood
By the long straight road where the Romans strode.
Up in Jolly Jack Wood the grandchildren stood
And the games they played as the tree trunk swayed
Recalled the climbs of the olden times.

Sam counted the rings on the trunks and things.
Ellen's broad smile made us dance for a while.
Ciara edged nearer where the leaves grew clearer.
Lulu and Roisin kept the branches in motion
Two of a kind with determined minds.
Chuckling Johnny, cheeks red and bonny,
Singing a song as we paddled along

In the mud and grass where the sandals passed
In an age long gone when the soldiers of Rome
Would rest on the hill as their children spilled
From the wagons to play on the tree trunk's sway
Finding acorns with roots where our Wellington boots
Would unearth the same in the years to come.

Christopher Payne

Chrysanthemums

The world has become darkly monochrome,
Birds grey as the grey skies fly with dead leaves
On the chilling wind through the raw damp air,
And pale mists to leafless trees grimly cleave.

It's November, heavy with lifelessness,
But the chrysanthemums are still in bloom
Just outside my front door like summer stars,
Shining gold defying the damp, dark gloom.

Shining even in the dour winter night,
Strangely luminous; they seem unaware
Of the dying year or the rain-blasted earth
In which they grow under the street lamp's glare.

The world has become darkly monochrome,
But the chrysanthemums are still in bloom . . .

Margaret Hibbert

Disaster Area

Frail ladies on rigid trolleys lay
And stare in resignation
At ceilings of fluorescent lights.

A thin plastic name band
Swims around a thin, bony wrist;
A glimmer of hope - the sign of admission at last . . .
But which day? Which week?
What bed?

Thirst beckons, but goes unquenched.
Stomachs cave in and grimace,
And pain swamps, unrelieved.

Others slump in varying weary
Posture, upon hardened plastic
Neon-orange chairs, designed
To torture.

The optimistic stay painfully seated,
Recalling the comfort
Of soft seats and home -
Yet willing such thoughts to evaporate . . .

There could be a painkiller
Or bandage,
In less than ten hours . . .

Groans.
Telephones, never stop.
Rushing feet and swishing
Starched aprons and cubicle curtains,
Glide, from side to side.

A lone white-coated man
On the run with mobile phone at ear
Rushes in.
Which patient might get lucky here?

Gabriela Alexander

TODAY'S IMAGES

Come fly with me above this land we love . . .
cliffs rise from rocky coastland dressed in green
and gold when sunlight glints on steel, now inland
city-bound, through grey-smoked clouds, we see
the urban tracts of peppered orange-brick
and shrub laced with spaghetti strings.

Close in to spot-check in this vast arena,
highlight opposing images that illustrate the year
2002 . . . will they remain awhile
rooted in this region's life, or disappear in history
files, like bath bubbles that fleeting cling
to soft wet skin? Tomorrow they may not last.

Here the maddening crowd, fresh-faced, leather-clad
scream for attention on waves of hysteria
following a football, and far from the maddening crowd
eagle-eyed ramblers tiptoe through leafy woodlands
stalking a shy tree-creeper.

There, traffic builds up around the tangled mass
of ripped metal and flesh, in a cordoned-off space
beyond the policeman . . . here the traffic concedes
to the stream of humanity, bare-legged, bouncing
past rows of spectators in marathon ovation.

While spasmodic forms, long-haired and glassy-eyed
in coloured flashing beams, sway stoned in the churns
of a rhythm-beater . . . beads glisten on temple, as trumpets
flare, descend in an ivory silence, holding listeners
spellbound in the wand-woven magic of sound.

Today's images may be served packaged,
bounced across a screen in a small cuboid
and viewed in colour.

Evelyn Leite

When I Die

When I die
Do not wear black for me.
Wear the colours of the rainbow;
The blue of sky and sea.
Remember I'm at rest now;
At peace forever more
And the colours of the rainbow
Find me dancing on the shore.

When I die
Sing no sad songs for me.
Praise the time we had together -
Sing songs full of glee.
Freedom comes to all who wait,
It now embraces me.
Let your voices ring out loud.
Be glad that I am free.

When I die
Do not wear black for me,
But the colours of the rainbow
Making me forever free.
And when you go into a room
And hear a little sigh
It's only me watching you
As gently I go by.

Always I'll be near to you
Watching what you do,
And deep within your memory
You'll know that I loved you.
So no more black and no more tears
Are you to shed for me
As always in your memory
I'll be forever free.

Shirley Woodbridge

SOLITUDE

I find solitude a blessing.
It gives respite from others' attention.
Solitude gives me a chance to reflect.
The stillness helps me to relax.
In relaxation my thoughts give rise to overtures of levity.
No interruption from outside influence.

I find solitude a soothing experience.
My recollections of the past manifesting as joyous reprises.
When I'm alone I find no distraction.
My mind can stimulate my very being.
In solitude the spirit must never descend to a lower level.
Use your isolation to lift that spirit to the heights.

I find solitude a breath of fresh air.
You can converse only with your inner self,
Leaving any intrusive commentators out of your spectrum.
Walking alone doesn't mean *being* alone.
Use your solitude as a barrier to inhibition.
Find your own level of expectation.

I find solitude a dreamer's paradise.
What you perceive in your mind you wish as a bounty.
You can experience a heartfelt fantasy,
The fantasy being a product of your imagination.
Only in solitude can your imagination run riot,
Giving you contentment and an insight of abounding pleasures.

In solitude peace of mind may come to the fore;
Use that solitude to lighten exasperation.
Then delve into your inner thoughts
And discover self regard.

W G Stannard

IMAGINATION

Suddenly the imagination flowers -
Transmuting roots, earth, dung and water
By secret alchemy to gold
Of fluted petals - an extravaganza
Of colours, shapes, scents - riotous, fantastic,
Springing, shooting, budding, bursting, blossoming,
Squandering seeds in wanton wastefulness -
Another universe, a new creation.

The spring is like a birthday -
A present wrapped in leaves and buds, until
The opening - and the inevitable surprise,
The grace of the expected miracle.

Deborah Maccoby

The Journey Of Life

Living a life isn't easy,
For life has many twists and turns,
It is an incredible journey,
With valuable lessons to learn.
When shadows arrive out of nowhere,
And a cast of dark clouds appear,
All of your troubles upon you,
Seem very loud and clear.
There's always a light after the shadows,
To lift you out of life's sorrows,
If you believe and have faith in your life,
There will always be a brighter tomorrow.
You only get one life,
And only one journey through it,
The requirements are quite simple,
If you put your mind to it,
Take life easy, live life to the full,
Don't let worry set in,
If you do this, that's when your troubles begin,
Be peaceful and good, believe in yourself,
And you'll find that life's long journey,
Is full of all the wealth that anyone could ever believe,
And then in life's great long journey,
You're very sure to succeed.

Toni Attew

Secret Retreat

As the river flows down the valley,
The leaves on the trees turn golden brown.
I have found my haven,
Somewhere to retreat to.
The birdsong happy,
The people friendly,
This is my home, my place to stay.

Emma Jayne Barker

The Ghost Of Anne Boleyn

Hush, did you hear that moaning sound
Amidst the rustling through the trees?
Can you hear a faint voice calling
Or is it just the wailing in the breeze?

Is it just the evening's moonlight
Casting shadows across the wall?
Only I thought I saw an outline
Of a woman moving through the hall.

You say it is the trick of night
Which casts shapes within my head,
But I swear, something just brushed by me
Where now only gallows' ravens tread.

Listen, don't you hear that wail
A trumpet's tooting drone,
Followed by drumsticks quickly drilling
And the thud of blade on bone?

Do these battlements and ancient bricks
From a time in years gone by,
Still hold its evil deeds in chains
Where the forsaken souls still lie?

A shadowy, drifting, lonely form
A clouded shape of sad decease,
Torn by an action so terrible
That it can never rest in peace.

A murmur, a faint whispering plea
Cries out from these walls within,
A sigh of injustice and betrayal
From the ghost of Anne Boleyn.

Carol Wilkins

POETRY

I have at my disposal an Alphabet
With which I can express this or that idea
Or train of thought.
Alternatively,
I can let the wind blow through it
And listen to the sound it makes.

Alan Wooding

Money, Money, Money

Although money has a major part
In life
There are things
That it cannot buy
Excess of it are always needed
To spend on sick and needy
So better share this
Without being greedy
The nature of money
Is to change hands quickly
Take care of it by being cautious
And a bit thrifty
So that it may bring happiness to you
And to others while you have it
It really matters
How you spend it
Let not all go
Save it for a rainy day or more
This simple method
Would leave a bank balance behind
Which gives an immense peace of mind
Money is the root of all evil, they say
That happen very often to many
When handled in an uncontrolled way
But it is a blessing to possess it
Then you need not stretch your palm to others
When you really need something
You spend happily on it

Kamala Perera

BEING AT PEACE

When seeking freedom from the cares of life
We're drawn towards the open countryside,
To roam around the gentle rolling hills
Or seek some solitude in ferny dells
Where tumbling streams pursue their merry way
In secret places underneath the trees;
Or maybe we escape to distant lands,
Traversing deserts canopied with stars,
To gaze above in wonderment and love
At those bright lamps that spin in endless space,
The multitudes that human eyes can scan,
Yet conscious of still more as yet unseen.
In places such as these we feel the peace.
Perhaps we choose the tropical delights
That can be found upon a palm-fringed shore
Of some deserted island in the sun,
To lie on soft white sand beside the sea
And listen to the lapping of the waves
That flow in rhythm and in harmony,
A place still unpolluted by mankind,
The busy world of commerce left behind
With all its diesel fumes and traffic jams.
If we could find the right environment
We think that we could always live in peace,
Yet finding peace despite the great demands
Within the working world and 'midst the roar
Of trains and lorries can be worth much more.

Anne Greenhow

WORDS

Flooding in
like water from broken rivers
desperate
searching for a place to settle
I listen sleeping
let them nudge their way inside
cheekily
in abstract moody disturbing dreams
I shake my head
to rattle them around
until they fall like crystals
onto the blank page

They push
shove, wriggle into natty dialogue
cloudy descriptions
rambling monologue
I am powerless
to hold them back (even if I wished to)
they pour out
jumping, leaping, screaming a way onto paper
onto screen, out of my
swimming head
and into something
readable, coherent, poetic

Rachelle Claret

SYDENHAM, LONDON, SE26 5HX

In 1920 when I was born the roads were lined with trees,
Sydenham was quiet and countrified with flowers, birds and bees.
Most food was then grown locally! Tradesmen brought it to the doors.
There were milkmen, butchers, fishmongers and grocer shops galore.
We paid in cash with Lsd. We lived in careful days,
but this was well before the war which came and changed our ways.

The Crystal Palace had been built high up upon the hill.
It had been most successful. Pre-war we had our fill
of various entertainment, music, strange animals and zoos.
I walked around the grounds and was frightened in the maze.
The firework show on Thursday nights we watched from far away,
but in '36 the Palace went, burnt out in a big blaze.

Once Sydenham shops were rather grand - assistants were polite.
To buy at Cobbs, Dewhursts and Boags was really a delight.
After the war these shops were gone, replaced by 'friends' afar.
They came from foreign places and made the High Street a bazaar.
No longer could you buy your clothes in comfort from big stores.
Sydenham had changed to little shops of knickknacks, food and flaws.

You have to go some miles away if big shops are required.
Buses are quite frequent, and there's not much room for cars.
Penge, Beckenham and Bromley are next places near around
where shopping can be done again in large stores which abound.
Sydenham's no longer as it was - it's changed in many ways
St Bart's is still up Westwood Hill - other churches Kent House way.
Some pubs remain, the cinema's gone, there seems nowhere to play.
Perhaps in time life will come back into this pretty place
that I remember years ago when Sydenham had some grace.

Doris E Pullen

A MINER'S LAMENT

I hear the voices and the sounds
Like distant whispers all around
Then stillness fills my silent room
No sound, no voices, I am doomed.

Nothingness comes over me
For there is nothing I can see,
And sadness fills my broken heart
For from this place I'll not depart

I hear sweet music playing
And loved ones faces do I see
But only in my mind's eye
And only in my dreams.

As I feel around these darkened walls
My thoughts begin to race,
And slowly do the pieces fall,
Like a jigsaw into place.

Never again to see the sunrise
Or to walk in meadows green,
Nor sit beside a babbling brook
Or see things yet unseen.

For this is now my resting place,
My catacomb, my tomb
And all the earth around me
Embraces like a womb.

And as I sit and wait for death
From this place I'll never go
For I have made my peace with God
One hundred feet below . . .

A Pope

Abney Park Cemetery (North London)

A shaft of light cuts through the trees
Old, crumbling gravestones
Look so grand and serene.
It would be so cruel to disturb them
Where they have lain for so long,
But can I just sit here amongst you
Be your guest for this afternoon.

It's not that I have nothing else to do
Or that time is not precious
For me who lives,
It's just that it feels so peaceful
And my head spins with the fastness of this world,
Perhaps I am getting old.

Or is the world getting faster
Faster than it used to be
Whereas you remain so still,
And peaceful and serene.
So I sit here amongst you
'Til my head feels more still,
Yet I must be getting back soon
To reclaim my place in the world
To run as fast as I must,
I wasn't made to give up.

You see, I don't want to be where you are
I just want to sit here amongst you
Be your guest for a while
For until my time is up
I'll gladly give up some time.

Maria Pelengaris

Celestial Queen

The moon, one brilliant circle of light
hangs teased by the scudding nebulae.
Veils gently brushing her face from sight
Melting into the 'Milky Way'

Appearing and disappearing into the night.
The clouds permit, then finally cover
this vision of loveliness shining bright.
Cherished and protected as if by a lover.

Cradles 'midst the heavens remaining unseen,
Her image effaced, only in the mind's eye,
She might never have been.
The clouds float on united across the darkening sky.

Dreams are carried up by the great God Aiolos,
On the wing of ethereal time.
Astral travelling, bridges to cross
Wafting on an invisible line.

The clouds they tire of flying together
and start to part as to nature they heed.
With purpose and swiftly, light as a feather,
They depart, for night will soon recede.

No sound to break the spell or jar
the wondrous sight before the dawn
of the sky that hints of another life.
Mortals sleep on!

A brilliant gem, light against dark blue,
The moon shimmers, intensely bright,
the mind to imbue,
Mortals sleep on!

Before such beauty one stands in awe
of the circle of perfection, devoid of flaw,
Mortals sleep on!

The scene starts to pale, inevitably sad
as the orb withdraws to herald the day.
Awake all mortals to the Aubade!

Daphne McFadyen

My Tall Ladies

They stand so elegant and tall,
And gracefully, they bow and sway,
Their composition, hearts enthral,
Their beauty's captured by the day.

Oh ladies fair, who wait to greet,
Look down, upon this face of mine,
Your countenance, I love to meet,
Your blossoms blush with pale carmine.

How sad to see you burdened so,
When evening storms have taken toll,
Your raindrop necklace stoops you low,
To kiss the mother of your soul.
Your beauty comes but once a year,
Midsummer brings that joyous time,
'My tall ladies' you appear,
As hollyhocks that stand in line.

How then have you acquired a name?
To link you with humanity,
It's my sentiment and aim,
To make you special, just for me,
    'My tall ladies'.

Margaret Nicholl

CHANGES

I cannot stop the dread
that wells up inside me
of things yet to come
and the changes yet to be

I cannot stop the course of time
and the things I don't know
I can however be positive
in order for me to grow

To be open to life's lessons
build my strength my mind
develop an understanding
of me and mankind

To constantly move forward
use the key for another door
can only prove positive
when learnt from lessons before

I cannot stop the changes
I cannot stop the dread
but by focusing on the good
I can change my attitude instead

Angelia Burke

LOVE TIMES TWO

Forever mindful
Of days past by,
    We met
    We laughed
You and I.
First spring
And rainbow skies.
    Warm light
    Warm love
Change two to one
    We cared
    We shared
What's done is done,
    Summer breeze
    And buttercup sun,
Deeper then
Our feelings went,
    Time apart was
    Time mis-spent
Hand on heart
Our vows intense.
Each fading year
Life loses bloom,
    We loved
    We dreamed
Old autumn's tune.
    Golden corn
    And harvest moon.
The landscape changed
But never us,
    With youth
    With age
Remained uncrushed.

Cold nor ice
Could not us rust,
We wintered over
With faith and trust.

Doreen E Millward

THAT SUNDAY FEELING

I too said Amen
In the sheep pen pugh
Surrounded by cardigans and woolly pullovers
Only to satisfy my kin
And maybe absolve myself from sin
If it's all true

I kneel for you
You at the front who clap
To the happy hymns
You at the back who nap
Saved from all your sins
By fiction

If what I say is untrue
Let us pray
And peace be with you.

Alexander Duncan

Bitter Regret?

In a world where old values are tossed aside,
what are our children to take as a guide?
TV tells us dollars and cents.
Fashion dictates girls should tighten their belts.
Studs through their noses and other places too.
Hair dyed in every shade - even orange and blue!
Tattoos where even men their anatomies hide.
Out of the window go morals, shame and pride.
Yet, even as I say this, there is good to be found,
gemstones of wisdom like rubies on the ground,
that I found, out in the East, when I was out there.
These 'gems' have more value than stones we can wear -
words of wisdom gently dropped from those who truly care.
We worry about all these jaunty young lives,
who one day will grow up to be husbands and wives.
Oh yes. It's nice to be unfettered and free.
Is it not better, in the years that lie ahead,
to have happiness instead of bitter regret?

Fuchsia Coles

THE TABOO

The audience cheer
As He toasts a life-long
Friend and enemy

This faithful ally
Who has stood by Him so many years
In a fruitful career

Spreading its cancer through the loyal host
Leaving only
The ugly behind

In endless ignorance
Friends offer the
Familiar aid

Whilst his family wait and wonder
Whether the poison has struck . . .
Once and for all.

Rachel Abbey

What Is Faith?

What is faith?
Some mysterious magic
That makes the
Impossible possible.

A rock to cling to
In stormy waters,
A promise to see the light
At the end of a very long, dark tunnel.

What is faith?
Trusting and believing
That you can still win the game
When the odds are heavily stacked against you.

Knowing defeat is but
An illusion
And that the darkest hour
Is always before the dawn.

What is faith?
The miracle of grace
That rewards the heart
That refuses to stop believing!

N Yogaraham

Don't Give Up

If only you knew
How much I know you
I see
  your beauty in your tears
    your strength in your weakness
      honesty in your silence and laughter
You don't have to try so hard
To be who you are not

Trying so hard to be perfect in an ugly perverted world
Shying away from what your heart truly desires and
Sheltering in the place you fear most.
Sanity, for you, is a loose thread
Wearing thin as nightmares become reality.
Reality is never what it appears to be
Only what you make of it
I understand yet I find myself so confused
My heart sinks when I hear you talk of
Tomorrow

Who knows what each day will bring
Be brave, my friend
 Our deliverer hears our every cry
  He is always there to listen to you
   His love outshines every problem, every fear
    Smile for me, my friend
     I want to see you happy again.
Your searching is not in vain
Whatever you want for the future has already been fulfilled
Your destiny is there for the taking
Believe it can happen and it will

My friend,
 Don't be afraid of the one who torments
  Instead have faith
   Faith is all we can rely on
My friend,
Turn your face to the Son
And the shadows will fall behind you.

Darlene Skeete

Hello Heathrow Harlington Bath Road Blues

Rush
    24 hour traffic nightmare
Push
    Through crowds going nowhere/anywhere
Wish
    As seconds pass - to be far from here

A sunrise over this beautiful concrete environment.
Aircraft dance in majestic movement.
As trees sway in gentle breeze, a father is born as a
Father dies amongst runways and houses touched by
Morning's golden light. All mirrored in a solitary gaze.

Grieving
    For a landscape born in time
                                        Fragile and yet real.
Forgiving
    The moment's escaping - revealing to conceal.
Living
    With ghosts of yesterday, as another plane flies away.

Nick Fryearson

My Dream

As I sat before the fire
In its warmth I began to tire
And as I drifted off to sleep
I had this wonderful dream to keep

I dreamt of a world completely at peace
Where all evil violence just had to cease
A wonderful happy land indeed
Where everyone had all they need

A world so full of smiling faces
Of all religions, creeds and races
A happier place you would never find
Where everyone is colour blind

Then I awoke to this world of today
And what I found I'm sorry to say
Is that the world I live in isn't quite fair
I awoke from that dream back into a nightmare

That dream of mine I still keep in my heart
And dreams can come true if we all play a part
After all we are humans no matter our colour or race
So let's make our world a wonderful place

W A Parham

CYCLAMEN

Diluted carmine butterflies
Transfixed by Ariel's breath,
A silent merry-go-round of shapes
Caught stilled in the moment of ecstasy
Drinking heavenly ambrosia from stems
Soft-delicately perched for one
Hesitant moment: frozen into petals
When on the point of fluttering off,
Caught so gracefully in the act,
Now set as living white flames,
Heating into pink flames, some of mauve,
A row of lamps to light the sill,
And set rubies and amethysts dancing
Against the outside English snow.
Oh, the magic of winter joy!

Do we dare to take our eyes
Away for a minute, lest
You flutter off? Where would you go?
To join your cousins in Iran?
Those wild but perfumed cousins,
Exotic gauzed floral nymphs?
Think not only of their charms,
Those ravishing dancing shapes,
Free-flowing fluttering figures
Caught on time's magic stems.

Ancient multitudes of ants
Marched with your most precious seeds,
Devout bearers of Royal treasure,
A 100,000 tenderly toiled;
From such microscopic activities
Erupted these exquisite emblems,
Spiralled stalks arise to breathe forth
Rubies, deep rubies, heart's blood
To baptise the pure white petals
With a delicate stream of heavenly love.

John Luke Rose

Staines Riverside

I sit on the bench, near the Thames
So calming, and peaceful it is
The river, could tell, lots of secrets
Of times gone by, I wonder why
There's a noise, to shatter my peace
A train goes, over the bridge

Rita Johnson

AWARENESS

The scent drifts, it hits my senses
I can feel the herbs penetrate my skin
I tingle with delight
I can hear my tastebuds popping in anticipation
I can see the steam rise and observe the droplets
I close my eyes and concentrate with all my might
In my hypnotic state I salivate
I can savour without ever opening my mouth
I touch the delicacy and let the sensation devour me
And step into the bath

Barbara Calvert

DERELICT

There you stand
Forlorn and cold
Open to the biting wind
Stripped and bare for all to see

Once you stood proud
Loved and warm
Your secrets hidden
By a cosy fire

But now who cares?
Who did this crime?
Who left you violated and undone?
Your secrets open to the rain and the sun
The laughter lingers, then fades and is gone.

Angie Fletcher

This Century

Through the centuries there have been men of vision
Creators of beauty, builders of future worlds.

But there are also men of war, not warriors in
Honourable battle. But abusers of power, who
Sweep through worlds, blind to beauty, propelled
By greed, bringing death and disease. Leaving
Destruction in their wake, for the peace makers,
Who spend a lifetime healing broken bodies and
Broken minds. They are compassionate. Men of peace.

In time to come, will this century be written in
Praise for man's greatest achievements or
Judged for destruction of our world.

N K Todd

CROYDON

Mammon grey and glassy staring
Stand the cliffs of Croydon town
Office blocks so vast, appearing
Ever set in moneyed frown

Shark wind blowing down the High Street
Clogged with bus and car and van
People hurry, must go quicker
Get there faster if they can

Whitgift shopping centre precinct
Modern style and prices too
Bargain sale! Come, two for one mate!
Lots of goods for sale to you!

Croydon East and Croydon West
Railways come and railways go
Helping move the people madly
Pushing ebb and pressing flow

Busy, busy Croydon town now
Suburb of suburbia
Who will love you, concrete Croydon
Vulgar, but vernacular.

Martin Harris Parry

Snow At Dawn

At last the apricot sun yawned into view
As the town lay softly sleeping,
All was strangely quiet,
Like a giant's secret keeping.

A gossamer thread had drawn its silver piece
Across the heavens - so jet,
And an unseen hand laid a treasured mantle
Into place, now gently set.

Each garden quite equal, in this glittering scene,
With boughs bent so low,
'neath the burden of snow,
Like beggars hunched tight in white sacks.

No dogs barking for walks in the park,
Only muffled, comfortable silence.

No clicks from the heels of the girls on their way to the station,
Missing too, the whistle of the boy who delivers the papers.
Where was the clink of the bottles on the step?
And the rattle of letters through the door?

The only sign of life was the paw prints
That showed in the crushed diamond spread,
Where a cat had loped home
From a night on the tiles and now was ready for bed.

Carol Middleton

DATING AGENCY

I gaze at you across the table - as the shadows fall
A little touch of candlelight lends magic to it all
And though we've only met tonight, I think we could get on
Tho' you're only one of many from the evenings that have gone

We're on our best behaviour - and dolled up to the nines
We've worked out all our strategies and both rehearsed our lines
But I'll tell you 'cos I like you and I think it's only right
- I may not always look as good - as I do tonight.

We're nonchalant and try to hide the longing to belong
Tho' the flesh is not as fresh nor the spirit quite as strong
My contact lenses and my teeth are perfectly in place
You look divine! You must have spent an age upon your face
And so, just for this evening, we'll forget about our ills,
Forget about the kids at home, the mortgage and the bills,
And maybe you won't really mind - though I thought you might
(that)
I may not always look as good as I do tonight.

Though I'm dressed up to the nines, I'm really not well off
I wake up in the morning with the wind and smoker's cough
Bleary-eyed and tousle-haired, with stubble on my jaw
I struggle out of bed and leave my socks upon the floor
And sometimes I am grouchy when it's raining and I'm tired
And people say I talk too much when tipsy - or inspired!
I've told you 'cos I like you and I hope that that's alright
I may not always look as good - as I do tonight.

That tired old dating agency that hides behind its doors,
The ones who gave their lives away upon a hopeless cause
And those who lost the brightest love they're ever going to get
And all those looking for a dream who haven't found it yet;
I hope they find them someone nice; the years go by so fast
There's so little time to build a love that's really going to last.
In the mirror our reflection is caught by candlelight
(but)
We may not always look as good - as we do tonight

Joseph Kilhane

DEPARTURE

Whilst the siren song of winter
spreads silently over abandoned earth
we tread carefully away to a different hearth.

The hovering of the last sparrow
casts shadows in its fine moment
above the glacial grass,
hinting at past futures.

Huge trees sway softly
in these sibilant winds.
Their hissing whispers temptations
renewing a sublime youth
of echoing memories.

Their branches curve,
a cursed witches' cauldron
brewing potions of storms,
before they become still.

But here, a solitary band of water
shimmers, as if it were a false vision of bright day
split asunder by boundaries of our two sides.

It is as death.

Meg Jefferies

The Quiet Shore

When the beach is empty and the incoming tide has
washed away the footprints of the daytime throng;
when the silent cliffs rise sheer and green capped
and the sun sinks low on the distant horizon,
splashing orange and red on the gently heaving waters,
then it is that the memories of past days and weeks and
years, drift across your mind and peace descends upon your soul.
Then it is that you may sit in silent contemplation,
while the evening breeze caresses your hair like the
gentle fingers of a benevolent God.
If an unpleasant memory should steal past that guardian
angel of peace, it will stay for but a fleeting moment,
then steal away before the quiet beauty that so fills
the soul there is no room for ugliness and you will rise
and walk along the quiet shore, back into the busy world,
strengthened and fortified by nature's own soothing balm.

P M W

HALF AN HOUR TO LANDFALL

Half an hour to landfall, near the Polynesian shore,
I'm stuck on a raft made of balsa wood with this Nordic type
named Thor.
He's a man with a chip on his shoulder, and a Kon-Tiki passion
to prove,
That across the Pacific long years ago, different tribes were
on the move.

Half an hour before landfall, and we've entered the Bay of Pigs,
Our objective is to oust Fidel, with his speeches, his beard and fatigues.
It's the new way of life we object to, and we're rooting for JFK,
We want to reopen casinos, bordellos and live the American way.

Half an hour to landfall, and we're going over the top,
So I'm all tanked up on whiskey, which I've guzzled like soda-pop.
Now an officer's waving his pistol, he's cursing and starting to warn,
If I don't get riddled in no-man's land, there's a chance I'll be
shot at dawn.

Half an hour before landfall, and I'm swimming with Chairman Mao,
I'm over with Nixon in China, he's determined the reds will kow-tow.
Tricky Dicky's suit is foreign policy, to his strong will we've all
got to bow,
Though I didn't quite fancy the effluent Yangtze, I took a dive to duck
a diplomatic row.

Half an hour to landfall, Saint Brendan recites a prayer,
While 4000 miles to the eastward, lies the coast of Kerry
and Clare.
We're about to discover America, though we didn't know that was
its name,
What a shame our trip's looked on as mythic, we won't sail into that
Hall of Fame.

Half an hour before landfall, my imagination soars,
To the southern seas with Captain Cook, and I'm drawing on the oars.
I was press-ganged into service, spent two years before the mast,
But I've learned to love life on the ocean wave and I try to forget the past.
We've made these exciting discoveries of land, and we're sure to make some more,
So I'm full of endeavour and resolution as we step on Hawaii's shore.

Half an hour to landfall, it's the time that I love best,
That tingle of excitement, my life a palimpsest.
There's a long long trail a'winding, I've been trekking the Golden Road,
When I finally stand in Samarkand, my new age will be one day old.

30 minutes to landfall could this be the time to strike,
When the heart is at its weakest, and all enemies look alike?
20 minutes to landfall, and I'm trembling on the brink,
And the blood is pounding in my ears and I'm scarcely fit to think!
Just ten minutes to landfall, it's too late now to retreat,
Though I'd like to reflect on the sunrise, and I've suddenly got cold feet.
But the landing craft's waiting to take me, to the shores of Gallipoli,
And a shrill inner voice is screaming at me, that this is the place where you'll die.

J D Farrell

THE BUCKET OF WATER

He came from a place where people walked in the rain,
He remembered holding out his hands when he was young,
he wanted to hold all the oceans in his hand,
But he really didn't understand where the rain came from.
So he went to school and asked his teacher . . .
He didn't know.
So he left school not seeing any reason to be there,
He travelled on the sea for many years,
Trying to understand the mystery of water.
Every time he picked it up, it ran out of the side of his hand.

He decided to buy a bucket and start a collection,
He placed his bucket out in the rain and watched the water
collect in it.
He was very happy sitting out in the rain,
He began to feel like water himself.

A tear fell from his eye.
He was beginning to understand the mystery of water.

He sat by the bucket for years, waiting for the rain.
He stopped eating, he was too absorbed in his bucket of rain,
That became a bucket of water,
He got thinner and thinner until he finally disappeared,

He had mastered the art of water.

He realised that capturing it in a bucket was not the answer.
He knew the answer, but by the time he knew, it was already too late,
He had gone back to the sea.

John Drake

DORSET SPRING

The rolling Downs of Dorset
Are home to many treasures
There's many an ancient Hillfort marks
The site of early man's endeavours,
And with 'Wessex' towns and hamlets
Of Thomas Hardy fame
A search reveals 'The Vale of Little Dairies'
Where youthful 'Tess' and soulful 'Angel' came.

Yet through the winding valley lanes
Where primrose speckled banks aglow
There lie the ancient stony bridges
Humpbacked to cross the watermeadowed flow,
While bluebells light the woodland scene
Cow parsley packs the open ground
Wild garlic scents the footpath track
So beauty lies for all around.

David Patrick

Advertisements

Going to school when I was a lad,
I could tell you the wording of every ad
That disfigured the hordings beside the road
Traversed by the tram in which I rode.

Now that I'm older I can shut my eyes
To ads on hordings, regardless of size,
And notices strictly forbidding me to
Do many things I've not wanted to do.

The TV adverts that offend my ear,
The DJs bring would-be's I don't want to hear.
They tell me the time to switch off and not on,
For who wants to listen to rubbish like yon.

Who are these folk who are trying to sell me
Things I don't want, upon the telly,
Useful page displays in every daily
And even in journals which publishers send me?

I notice the girls, their charms displaying,
While set virile men like asses, braying.
But what's being said in the caption below,
Like everyone else, I don't want to know.

When will foolish ad men realise that we,
Just want some hard facts, so we can all see
For ourselves why their goods should attract us,
The girls and hyperbole only distract us!

Walter Dalton

Winter Day

The moors are black this winter day
Grass blighted beneath sweeping winds
Past times frozen far beyond
Imagination's furthest leap.

Here and there birds' voices
Break the bare moorland silence
Where are the wild rabbits?
They stir the shadows of the night.

Let the dark days turn
And the ditches dry on burning sand
That evening hoot rising from the hills
No one is there but the sailing windmills.

Down tracks over the singing falls
Where a mesmerised clumsy cloud clutters
An ambling, slithering blotched hour
Stumbles down through the dark.

This is the familiar path to the white meadow
A narrow pass that ends in nowhere
Abandoned on snowdrifts
The magenta glow of coming summer.

Daisy Abey

The Lull

Observe the river through the haze
Glimpse a kingfisher's orange blaze
Reed beds conceal a dragonfly
Until the sun relights the sky
The gudgeon makes a lazy leap
Then disappears to waters deep
Nervous fieldmice scamper to go
Beneath a tree felled long ago
Restless clouds above fields of corn
Stage nature's prelude to a storm

Tedward

A LAMB OF THE ARK

A sense, a feeling, tells me to go
To leave my home and mother.
My father, all my friends and food,
Each sister and each brother.

A male lamb trots by my side
And through the woods we trail.
Until we reach a stretch of land
To stop staring, we fail.

A boat, big enough for two
Of each animal, each thing
And on the boat we climbed
Happiness to bring.

What seemed like forever
We travelled in this boat,
With each and every tiger
And fox and billy goat.

And soon the sun came out
And cleared the darkest sky
A rainbow as a promise came
Glinting in each owned eye.

The flood evaporated
And soon the grass lay green,
We freed ourselves in pleasure,
New corn, new crops, new scene.

The male sheep and I gave birth
To six precious young sheep,
The beauty of this new world
Enough to make us weep.

Claire Proctor (11)

BROKEN DREAMS

Does the old familiar path still wind
  Across the distant hill?
Flanked by purple columbine
  And wild daffodil?
Does it lead to the hidden vale
  Beyond the ferny hill?
Across the mossy dale
  And the twisting, fingered rill?
Does the watchful hawk still soar
  High above the trees?
Above the tarn and tor -
  On a warm summer breeze?
Does the sacred oak still stand
  That marked a lover's tryst?
And is the glade by the strand
  Sheathed still in evening mist?
Are the woods still verdant aisled
  Paths of sheer delight?
An emerald palace where beauty dwelt -
  And my heart was so beguiled!

Tell me: do the dead leaves of winter
  Still rustle on frozen ground?
And is the mantled snow so deep
  As to muffle every sound?
Does the ice-bound rill await
  The warm breath of spring?
And does the tarn below the tor
  With deathless memory cling?
Does the dusk still call to shadows
  Drawing them ever near?
Where once in vanished summer
  The skies had shone so clear!
And from the sacred oak
  Does there drift a piping call?

A note that is sad and long . . .
  As if a spirit was held in thrall?
And high in the leafless branches
  Does there sit a solitary bird?
And is it from the sacred oak
  That the throstle's call is heard?
Does he cock his head and listen
  Yet never a reply is made?
Do the calls of anguish continue
  Across the frozen glade?

Derek Budd

ADMIRATION

Glowing like a bright star in the dark night,
I could gaze up at thee for hours and hours,
Stare at thy guiding and undying light,
More I look, the more darkness devours.

How can I ever let pass a whole day,
Without thy beautiful self by my side?
Without thee, I too shall perish away.
I must tell thee, that to save thee I tried.

Like a kind mother watching your babes grow,
Thy eternal kindness to all thou givest.
Thy sweet smell like that of a deep red rose,
Forev'r in my heart thou shalt livest.

On thy grave it shall never ever rain
And thy beauty shall never ever wane.

Claire Keoshgerian (13)

Grandma's Brew

A summer garden perfumed with sweet aromas,
Distinctly dominant, prevails the fragrant mint I recall so well,
The invigorating aroma lingers, arousing my innate senses,
Awakening nostalgic memories, of childhood days gone past,
Charmed by this exquisite aroma, reunited again at last.

Grandma's mint plant, growing vigorously wild,
Her tea brewed to perfection, cure for an ailing child,
Grandma's discreet magic brew, never failed to work,
The minty aroma, blended with passionate tales she told,
Huddled abound the fireplace, sheltered from the cold.

The fragrance wraps itself around me, in this garden of time,
Lost in sentimental memories, with this everlasting mint of mine,
Inherited from Grandma along with her secret recipe.
My daughter sits nearby, nursing a wounded knee,
Time now to gather some fresh mint, to brew Grandma's tea.

Vilma Whittle

The Little Church Among The Trees

Saint Andrew's Church in Frimley Green
For 50 years my joy has been,
My refuge too in grief profound
Where sorrows are with mercies crowned.

'The little church among the trees'
My children named this place of peace.
This place of prayer and melody,
Of friendliness and harmony.

The lychgate shelters all from rain,
And plaques of bronze record the names
Of gallant heroes of the wars
Who gave their lives in freedom's cause.

In springtime still the daffodils
Proclaim new life, and pleasure fills
Our hearts, and hope of balmy days
Inspire the spirit with God's praise.

And then, through summer, roses red
And pink and golden fill the beds,
Where shining plaques remind us too
Of loved ones now at rest with you.

In autumn time the beeches glow
With gold and bronze; and winter's snow
Adorns the pine trees and the yews,
Like Christmas cards with joyful news.

The seasons of the Christian year
Are celebrated with good cheer.
Christ's birth at Christmas, Easter's bliss
And harvest's store of plentiousness.

O little church among the trees,
You never fail my heart to please.

Nancie Cator

LATE BEE

Twosomes of evergreens smirk to themselves
As the last colours of warmer months expire.
Boasting to their under evolutionised kin
Who do not own the intelligence of conclusive deathlessness,
And perhaps do not want to.
But it is still feasible to forbear their green eyes,
Pinched out in the rearmost browning moments.
However, the late bee can be heard laughing too.
Only out of timidity fruiting from famine.
Best stay questing low to the ground.
Intermiss your wings on occasion and dissipate your senses.
Reveal the scent of your animation and career.
For any blooms that you fertilise now will in turn become behind.
Catering a salvation for next year's late entrances.
Unknowing but epochly making you a hero,
Sanctioning undeserving misfortunates a flourishing oath.

Beverley Joyce Cope

JAZZ . . .

(Mr Oscar Peterson)

The trumpeter commences a theme
bassist and drummer set the scene;
a master of keyboard pyrotechnics
the virtuoso pianist skilfully picks
up the melody. Cool, sharply pert,
the musicians tantalize and flirt
with the pitch, finally producing
the rhythm of matchless swing.
Incandescent razzmatazz -
well that's jazz!

Sheila O'Hare

HACIENDA PARADISE

Lazing in her softly padded chair
The sun warms her aching limbs
She barely hears the balmy sounds of summer
Surrounding her Hacienda Paradise.

The sweet intoxicating mix of sun and wine
have made her drowsy.
Her mind wanders aimlessly through an alleyway
of forgotten memories.

She slowly turns her head to a scene between two
gently swaying branches revealing a moving picture show.
The sea gives a responsive view of diamond spangled waters
glistening in the sunlight.
She looks up to the sky that has been painted with a majestic hand
sweeping across a canvas with careless accuracy.
She is content, she closes her eyes, her mind and inhales her
Hacienda Paradise.

Susan Orr

Birth To Death

While a baby's waiting to be born
He's in a trance-like floating state of peace.
A place for his soul's transition
From the heavenly world he has so lately left.

At birth, his soul feels desperately sad,
Trapped once again inside another human frame.
He cries and wails - he cannot stand this new imprisonment.

God, in his mercy, lets him sleep for almost all the time
At first, to ease his new descent into this world.
Once again, as many times before, he gradually feels
Less and less distressed, and grows accustomed to his earthly state.
He takes his comfort from the human beings around him,
Who give him love and warmth,
And month by month, and year by year, he adapts to life on earth.

Until he's seven, he still retains some glimpses of his recent time
In heaven.
He even sometimes sees those he was with so recently.
His elders see and hear him talking to these friends, and say
'Just his imagination - he'll grow out of it one day;
Yes, it's sad to say - he surely will.

And so he grows, and once again goes through his time
Of learning here on earth - sometimes happy, sometimes sad.
Until once more, and in old age, his time to go draws near.
His soul prepares him once again, to leave this school of life,
And with a soft sigh of relief, at last, at last,
He reaches once again his heavenly home.

Betty Farajallah

Sunset Harbour

Boats sleep peacefully as night is near,
The light is fading as the sun goes down.
The sun projects its reflection onto the gentle waves,
The boats float gracefully as swans on a lake.

The small rowing boats dance in the fading sunlight,
The sound of waves relaxing like a gentle lullaby.
The pure fresh smell all around,
Like the sweet scent of daffodils on the ground.

The smoke from the boats rising into the air,
Everyone around is without a care.
There is the sight of land in the distance of the night,
The whole harbour a breathtaking sight.

The water is silk all around my fingers,
As the smell of sea air lingers.
This harbour is all the above,
And as beautiful as a dove.

Michelle Woodley

VALENTINES

(For Yolene and Charlotte Wisby)

Valentines is a day of love,
The bird of peace, of care,
The dove.
It flies through the windows of your soul,
To help your heart reach its goal.
What you desire, need and wish,
Can all be given in one kiss.
If the one true love can heed your dreams,
Help your thoughts, make your heartbeat seem,
Like an endless drum for a marching band,
When your hand is in my hand.
Then this love is the one for you,
And nothing else will ever do.
So when the one you love with all your heart,
Says they never want to be apart,
Hold them tight and let them know,
You'll never ever let them go.

Emily Burgess

THE CHANT OF THE PIED PIPER

Come little children everywhere,
Don't be afraid because I am there.
All the things that you've ever dreamed for,
It will all come true if you just follow me.

You could have, pizza and chips every night,
and stay up late until it's light.
You could play on the PlayStation all day long,
and tell parents and teachers what's right and wrong.
All these things that you can do,
Just listen and read and they'll come true.

No more school ever again,
You could even fly a plane
Sweets, sweets, every day,
The more you eat, the longer you'll stay.

Now you know what you can do
Come and join us,
Why don't you?

Rachel Beresford-Ward

A Special Question

W hy is a question I often keep asking, because
I know our love is everlasting
L ong ago when we were young
L ove was ready, but we were not.

Y ou and I have always shown
O ur friendship grows stronger as time goes on, as
U nderstanding each other's needs is never in question

M y love for you will never die
A love like ours is not a lie
R are it is, but we can prove
R eal friendship, love and honesty will win through
Y ou are confused and I can't help, although

M y head and heart both shout
E ternal love is what we have, and time alone will prove just that.

Joan L Munns

WORKING WITH YOU

Now that time has gone, flown away
it leaves space for another rainy day.
As I watch as the rain falls down I'll think of you,
and all the mad times that we have been through.
In the rush and in the slow,
teaching me all the things you would know.

You took me in when I had nowhere to go
showing me places to and fro.
Helping me through bad times and good times
which is why I keep making these rhymes.
So now we have to say goodbye,
I'm sure nobody will cry.

So goodbye to you
because all of our times are through.
Farewell to bad customers and all their complaints
because as you know
I have to go.

Tika (15)

HE IS OUR GOD

He is our God
Lord Jesus Christ our Saviour
He's Lord and King
Of all things great and small
So let us praise
And give Him all the glory
And tell the world that He is Lord of all.

The world should know
'Twas He who died to save us
None can deny
He gave His life for all
His precious blood
Was shed to save us sinners
It is His love that lifts us when we fall.

In gracious love
He draws us to the Father
And leads us gently
To our Heavenly home
When this life ends
We'll be with Him in glory
And there proclaim that He is Lord of all.

Peggy C

Bereavement

Bereaved, I faced a life alone,
Except for my son in Surrey,
And failing health increased my woe;
My life was one of worry.

Depression affected my lonely thoughts;
There were problems enough for solution,
But a move to the south to be near my son
To recovery made contribution.

A retirement flat became my home
Amid folk with similar feelings,
And I soon began to feel revived
By the power of friendly meetings.

My dearest wish would always be
To have my wife back with me,
But failing that, an impossible dream,
I'll settle for neighbourly comp'ny.

R T Walker

LIVING WITH FEAR

Is a life worth living
When nothing's going right?
Your dreams turn into nightmares
So you stay awake all night

Is a life worth living
When you always feel alone?
No one wants to talk to you
Not even on the phone

Is a life worth living
When you feel you just can't cope?
And other people laugh at you
As if you were a joke

Is a life worth living
When you just can't wait to die?
Hoping there's a heaven
Way up there in the sky

Is a life worth living?
Oh! I really wish I knew
'Cause this is how I see my life
Do you have the same life too?

Andrew F White

AUTUMN

Red, russet leaves,
Golden leaves,
Brown leaves in the fall,
Footsteps, yells, of children heading home for autumn season.

Hot cocoa, warm beds,
Autumn dreams dancing in their heads,
Chilly breeze, smoky breath,
Boots to warm their icy feet.

Creatures hibernating,
Sleeping safe and warm,
From squirrels, to fieldmice,
Every animal big and small.

Sleeping houses beyond the skies,
Oranges, reds, pinks, each one to catch your eye,
Grey smoke, wafting from the chimney tops,
This is autumn at its best.

Rosanna Jeffery

My First Someone

Do you remember my love, when we had it all?
So high up and then to fall
But something there was never right
If only we could have seen the light

We could have started oh so strong
Our love would have lasted oh so long
Deep deep down inside of me
I'm glad that you and me are free

I'm so glad that I had you
At the time nothing could have been more true
But something happened along the way
We drifted apart day by day

You'll always be a part of me
All I am, all I'll be
Where we've been and what we've done
I'm glad you were my first someone

Caroline McDougall

Harsh Truth

Nature's green grass
Against the harshness of
Dark human asphalt
Accentuates the differences
Between me and you

Natalie Sloper

The Basket Of Dreams

From the verge of the woven basket of dreams; I see
An intertwining delight of nature's craft
Set on hills and heights of delight
Depths and valleys pronounced
Surrounded round about by fields and trees

Over this dream of winding twigs and lanes
In greens and browns of nature's natural hues
Is the covering of sunlit glinted skies
Singing birds of promise gliding past
In praise of the beauty beneath their wings

Within the basket of dreams
Are orchards and greens
Sands of time holding in their cupped hands; rivers and streams
Trees wave along winding roads
Lanes, holding hands with fields e'er green
Leading to the heart of dreams

On the south and north within
Patterned streets making way for to see
The glint and slant of rooftops
Peering amongst treetops dense
Standing within and without valleys and hills

Making melody in the winds on the sides of it
Colourful flowers kissing; lending sweetness to the breath of it
Whistling amongst the winding twigs of it
To the depths thereof, beauty past compare
The woven hands of nature's song;
In the basket of dreams

Patricia Aboagye

Heavenly Twins

Oh, beautiful Selene, goddess of the night
You lay upon velvet sheets of midnight blue
Diamante stars sparkle through your flowing tresses
Your pale light shines as a beacon
Through the long hours of darkness
Until dawn's early light paints the awakening skies.

You slip behind a cloak of pearly clouds
To watch as Phoebe spreads her golden fingers
Caressing the land with warm kisses
Carried on nature's breath.

Trees stand tall and lift their arms
To greet the new day
Their leaves, a canopy to filter sunlight
To dapple dancing waters below.
Flowers blossom and raise their heads
To catch Phoebe's smile
Their perfume lingers on the gentle breeze.

As time passes and the day ages
Phoebe seeks her rest.
You awaken, sweet Selene, once more
To watch as Mother Earth rocks nature's cradle
In peaceful, dreamless sleep.

Carole Harradence

WALES

Buildings of stone, roofs topped with slate
Blackened cottages burned down with hate.
Lungs filled with songs, some filled with grime
Some Sundays the landlord does not call 'time'.

Druids and fluids in whiskered men's glasses
Bracken and heather and glacial passes.
Rivers go winding through valleys so deep
Whilst antics are played by never-ending sheep.

Scars on the mountains leave scars on the mind
Quaint seaside towns that time left behind.
Whispers in language kept just for the few
Secretly cursing unnoticed say Duw.

Rocks inside water, water in rocks
Pebbles and blue stone, houses of blocks
Of the wonderful granite and chimneys with smoke
Hair dark and curly - secretive folk.

Castles and follies, where Arthur once dwelt
Gwain and Glyndawr and the Prince of Wales knelt
Down to give his allegiance to Dai bach's homeland,
Land of my fathers where industry planned

The days of the miners, quarrymen, bards
Stones built in circles, split into shards
To make 'gifts from Llandudno' to take home to Mam
To put on the dresser and continue the sham

Steam trains and windmills and nuclear power
Idris's café and the daffodil flower
David and Dyfed, Bethel and Gwent
Mumbles and jumbles where money is spent

To eke out the giro at Aberafon Beach
To dream about holidays right out of reach
Of the Cardigan shoppers in Oxfam sweaters
And the Saturday riskers, losers and betters.

From Chester to Holyhead, Wrexham, Porthcawl
The wonderful mixture, not true Welsh at all
But Lancashire lassies, moved down for the air
Ladies from Leominster, play landladies there.

Others from Bristol, from Devon, from Hull
Bright ones and smart ones, lively and dull
All find the magic, which conjures up tales
Of the wonderful, marvellous mystery called Wales.

Elizabeth Williams

CANCER POEM

She was 22 and a quarter,
The night she passed away.
It was killing her inside
But she was living for each day.

He'd just passed 51,
When he took his last breath.
The years of treatment he'd endured
To postpone his death.

The baby was just seven months,
When she shed her last tear.
Born, diagnosed and died
All within one year.

He became a great grandad
Two months before.
If only he had known
What his life had in store.

She was due to start Uni
When she kissed goodbye to life.
Gone, are all her hopes and dreams
With her troubles and her strife.

It creeps up on you.
Consumes you in one bite.
Attacks you without warning.
Doesn't stop for day or night.

Few escape its terror,
Without a lasting effect.
Hard to find a reason why,
Even harder to detect.

It does not discriminate
Between black and white.
It spares the life of no one,
However hard you fight.

What an achievement it would be,
To contribute one suggestion,
That would help find an answer
For our long-standing question.

The urgency for a cure,
Would take too long to say.
For here's a disease we can't combat
And people die from every day.

Nicola Guest

Early Morning In Fueterventura

The cool chill of the morning, a blissful balm,
Before the fiery flame of the orange orb burnt down.
Stillness and serenity giving a pervading sense of calm,
The whispering wind being the sole solitary sound.

Standing strong on tall, thick elephant skin trunks,
Sturdy palm trees straight in the breeze.
Each supporting a pirouetting plumage drunk,
Of bright green fan-shaped leaves.

As the wandering wind rustled and rushed through,
The green finger-like fronds did prance.
Wildly blowing and fluttering as they blew,
Caught in a graceful, inescapable dance.

Wispy white clouds scudded past,
Racing off to an unknown destination.
Somewhere secret over the ocean vast,
To join forces and develop a meteorological creation.

In the sky, wider grew the patches of blue,
Allowing the sun's rays to shine bright.
Enhancing the bright colours of the bloom's hues,
Bathing the white-washed walls in searing sunlight.

A lone white seagull did effortlessly glide,
Over the smooth, still, sapphire sea.
Focusing for fish in the turn of the tide,
As shoals swam beneath the surface silently.

Ripples for waves lapped the golden sand,
Otherwise the sea of glass lay still and serene.
No splashing, no sandcastles, no bodies tanned,
Only the undisturbed, tranquil beach to be seen.

Mountains burnt and barren, highlighted the horizon,
Dusty with dirt tracks and not a shade-giving tree.
Heralding the heat of another day to come,
The early morning coolness soon to be only a memory.

Sally Fleming

WHAT LIES BENEATH

The surrounding sea lies like a terrific topaz,
White horses glide, gallop, jump and spring.
The bay is as calm as a millpond,
As the blue turning tide slips slowly in.

Ravenous ripples lap and lick the sulphur gold sand,
Whilst swim various fluttering fish.
Deliciously deeper lie multicoloured creatures
Their turquoise tails twirl, pirouette and swish.

When channelling deep, deep down into the murky depths,
The ragged rocks ominously sit.
Within the boulder's wide open mouth,
Is a putrid, petrifying black pit.

Silver striped scarlet fish sweep silently by,
One showing off its authentic head-dress.
It swivels and swings and spins around,
The silent seabed its fins do caress.

Beautifully banding the magnificent ocean wide,
Is colourful coral you cannot trust.
All pretty pinks, electric blues and graceful greens,
But arc horrifically harmful if against them you brush.

On the smooth and sandy ornamental ocean floor,
Sits an odious octopus, long legs knotting.
The slow waiting water swirls around
A sunken ship that is long forgotten.

Suddenly all the sea creatures look stunned and startled,
Quickly they scoot and scatter away.
A sly, swift shark swims round the corner,
Razor-sharp teeth showing, searching for precious prey.

It's not all beauty that lies beneath,
Evil and terror lurks there too.
Perilous predators and the poisonous coral reef,
Are hidden in the ocean blue.

Rebecca Fleming (12)

INVIGILATION

Silence

The single student turns the page;
She tours the questions in her mind,
Planning the route where interest leads,
Aborting journeys just begun
Or travelling boldly to the end.

She takes her pen, and suddenly
Rivers of liquid language flow;
Her racing thoughts direct their course
Towards the ocean of her words
To tumble into deeper sense.

I watch her write: slim fingers wield
The pen which shapes her answers now,
Black hair cascades about her face,
Dark eyes hide secrets of her mind;
Will she and Shakespeare think as one?

I have to warn her of the time.
She bites her lip in faint alarm,
And hastily concludes her work,
Arranges pages one by one,
Presents to me her finished text.

The script at last is packed away,
A stranger's eyes will scrutinise
And judge her efforts - pass or fail -
Assign a grade to change her life
For ever, at a God-like stroke.

She shyly smiles and leaves the place
That was her world that afternoon,
Too late now for second thoughts,
She steps into the sunlit street
To eight weeks of oblivion.

Sylvia Herbert

Before And After

Anxiety of mind but body sound
Yet, within an hour
The other way around.
Through a haze of dopey sleep
A montage of noises percolates the deep.
It seems to join as one within the pain
And blend together to become the same.
A call, a bang, and kitchen clatter,
Comings and goings
And constant chatter.
The touch of unseen hands,
The closing of a door,
The tap, tap, tap of heels upon the floor.
The rough brush of unfamiliar sheets,
And a shaft of light that breaks into a moving pattern
As it creeps
Across the void and gloom
Which, on a sudden
Has become a room.
And far away I hear the steady flow
Of traffic coming from a place below . . .

So -
Whilst body, mind and time
In limbo hang
Reality and I return
- To where this all began.

Frances Phillips

Untitled

As if to be floating on gentle waves
Instead of suffering thunder
Accepting the comfort of your own warm cloud
No longer being worn as a crushing shroud

Hours and days having meaning
No more the horrors of waking and sleeping
The terror of moving
My hands, my head, my eyes

Instead, wanting to look
Wanting to see
I think, I now am able to
Be me

Kim Quinn

Why I Didn't Do My Homework!

Wind gushing through my hair,
Weeping willows hang in bridal veils
Daffodils, swaying suns,
Scampering squirrels playing in bare trees.

Wandering pigeons with multicoloured waistcoats,
While the beaming sun shines down on me
The trickling river flowing aside of me
Punishing the rocks as it goes.

Swans gliding through the river, round and around
Birds singing all around
Bees buzzing, squirrels playing
Like children in the park.

Sara Miller (9)

My Heaven

Blue sky's Heaven
- that's what I believe
Green grass, sparrows singing in the trees
Warmth and sunshine with a gentle breeze
Balmy summers with the bizz of bees.

Summer's where my Heaven is
Spring is 'on the way'
Autumn's like an artist who is painting out the day.
It's winter when my heart grows cold;
The pilot light goes out
Unless it's crisp and sunny
I'll be sad or full of doubt.

So hurry hopeful springtime and
On to Heaven roll
To take me out of winter;
From this dark and dreary hole

I just can't wait for Heaven
To be with God's only Son
To spend all of eternity
With Him, the Glorious One.

In Jesus Christ there is no dark
Because He is The Light
And so I wait for Heaven's son
To make my sunshine bright.

Helen Anne Watt

ALONE

On a day alone like this
I reminisce the time your soft lips I would kiss,
The texture, the softness, the feel of your touch,
Something in my heart I truly miss so much,
I think of you and your beautiful son,
It's then I realise that I'm the stupid one,
I lost you both and my heart turned to stone,
But there's no one to listen cos all I do is moan,
All alone, no friends, no love, just me,
Sometimes, somebody else I wish I could be,
I hate my life so much right now,
People tell me it will change, but how?
They say I have to do it alone,
I do everything on my own,
Because,
I am all alone.

Bradley Reid

NIGHT MAGIC

Cool, calm, heavenly night,
With myriads of stars,
Twinkling ever so bright -
And the large silver moon
Chasing shadows with light -

Bathing in magnificent silvery sheen,
Mountain, wood and meadow green,
Making us with strange delight -
Feel the wonders of the night.

Mary Fitzpatrick-Jones

STAR FOLLY

(Dedicated to Henry Goodman, Louise Gold, Joan Savage, Myra Sands and the cast of the Royal Festival Hall revival of the musical Follies)

Some say this cast
Are not great big stars;
But test their mettle,
Give them a chance,
See them sing and dance.

Some say this cast
Are not great big stars
But they've talent enough any day,
And who wants a show sold
On big names anyway.

Some say this cast
Are not great big stars
But I'll route for them
Some of whom are a gem
After all I'm one of their fans.

Yes, some say this cast
Are not great big stars
But God damn it I'll settle
For *Goodman* and *Gold*
And *Savage* and *Sands*.

Emma Dorothy Shane

DOLPHIN SUNSET

Gliding silently over the water
Making no noise at all
Silhouetted against the sunset
Can you hear its soft call?

Red, yellow and orange
Are the colours I see
A shadow in front of the sun
It's waiting for you and for me.

I go to follow this creature
Hypnotised by its gaze
It swims into the horizon
Leaving me behind in a daze.

I feel all dizzy and shaky
The shadow is still there
Do I go with the mystery creature
To prove that I really do care?

It's beckoning me forward
So as I start to get near
I realise it's a dolphin
I'm no longer filled with fear.

I've always loved these creatures
But now it's swimming away
I think I've lost my chance
To get near a dolphin and play.

Hannah Bristow (10)

GOLDEN JUBILEE YEAR (2002)

G reat historical occasion,
O ur Queen's 50th year of reign.
L oyal to duty and to nation,
D evoted mother just the same.
E ndurance throughout duration,
N ow 76 years of age.

J oyful celebrations was our aim,
U mbrellas often used throughout.
B ig shows and the Commonwealth Games,
I n Manchester; spectators shout.
L ovely friendly people became,
E ager to see the Queen about,
E njoying the Royal parade.

Y oung and old all enjoyed the scene,
E very flag waving on her way.
A ll had a chance to see our Queen.
R oyalty really made their day.

Doreen Ranson

WAS I LUCKY?

Three score and ten ago.
White crosses, fresh in a row.
Red blooms flourish in the killing ground.
Was that a whistle? No, not that sound!

Memories with grief and tears.
Alone with thoughts of those years.
My friends gone, some found, some not.
Ashes to ashes, is that all they got?

All my dreams are blood.
With noise, fear and mud.
Was God with me? In that hole.
A non-existence, keeper of my soul.

Rain-drenched horrors abound.
Does death make a sound?
Will I ever lose this hate?
Don't know, what is my fate?

Life goes on they say.
Day after day, after day.
This life is bleak and tiring.
Listen! Can you hear the firing?

Will I ever find peace?
One day, this will cease.
All sunshine, no more dark pain.
Walking with my mates again.

Will it be paradise?
Is my soul that price?
To be in Hades I can bear.
As I've already been there!

Brett Lovett

Cardboard House Girl

She hangs on to her pots and pans
Her worldly possessions
That's all she has. Howling storm
Destroys her cardboard house.

The cardboard house girl,
Born poor, lives in poverty and scarcity.
It was not by choice, simply the destiny.

From the begin of beginning
It is the same kind of a day,
Tired and hungry, every day.
Forever shackled in a closed door.

Inside and outside, society, the way it is
As it has been, as she knows, as she sees,
The way she remembers,
She shivers in cold.

Morning comes, another day dawns
Nature's regular chores. She yawns.
It hurts to cry and it's insane to feel insecure.

She feels pain all over, stomach aches.
Delirious mind she feels poisonous snakes
Choking her. Pay back time is now.

All her dues are paid.

Stagehands put all the lights on, it's blazing
She enters amidst the applause, bells ringing.
Dressed in princely clothes and tiara on her head
She walks majestically through the open door.

Somen Sen

The Chiltern Hills

From Thames up to Bedfordshire is where they can be found,
And these hills from the east they rise gently from the ground,
With wondrous western limit stood high and proud aloft,
An escarpment high above a wet plain so soft,
For those who seek to find the edge of this precipice,
Breathtaking views of sunset shadows cast o'er abyss.

There's water in the south of this paradise of hills,
The Thames flows by from its source to ocean of no frills,
While in the north, the canal has cut and dug its route,
Summit up among the hills flows north and south to suit,
Trains from Paddington and Euston go by these enclaves,
While Marylebone and St Pancras take office slaves.

These hills, they are ancient from an ice age they were formed,
Each row of hills precisely with valleys quite adorned,
With trees and roads quite straight, while brooks keep pastures green,
There is barely any road which connects in-between,
And there are deep down bottoms, with roads so very steep,
Where water is extracted from chalk wells, oh so deep.

Amongst the hills are big towns where very many go,
Like Tring, High Wycombe, Amersham and Marlow,
There are small towns too and a stockbroker belt as well,
And myths of the countryside that people there dispel,
It's a rural area of green and pleasant hills,
A walker's wonderland to climb and then walk downhills.

It's an isolated world so near and yet so far,
Gentle and surreal life divining though not debar,
A wonderful oasis that's not far from London town,
When you come out from the city dawn until sundown,
There's museums, hotels and all you need to stay,
When it comes time to leave, you'll not want to go away.

J Lowndes-Yates

MIST

I am trapped in this place. This darkness.
The air fills with mist and I cannot see.
I cannot breath.
Drowning in a sea of pain.
I am alone. Alone in darkness.
It follows me, haunts me, mocks me.

I feel your acid kiss.
A numbing pain inside my head.
I hear your cruel laughter.
Voices echo inside me.
I stare out across the violet sky.
A swell of fear grips me.
A storm draws close.
Something smashed. Fragmented into a thousand pieces.

It calls out to me.
This black wave, a wave that consumes me like the ocean
against the sand.
The pain comes back. Sweeping through me like wind across
a deserted beach.

The sand chokes me.
I see nothing.
The mist grows dense
Slowly blinded by the blackness.

It grips my ankles with a sharp ache.
Glassy eyes stare up at me

I see her now. She is not what she seems, faint, distant.
She embraces the darkness.
Seduces me
Caresses me.
Not long now. Terror consumes my heart.
She rejects the artificial.

A chill, spills down my neck. I feel her presence.
Does she want me?
I cannot breathe. My lungs fill with the oily darkness.
I am calm,
Tranquil
Can she protect me?
I hear their cruel laughter. Louder and louder.

A crystal breaks. Blood runs from my eyes. I taste its bitter sweetness on my tongue.
Nothing but mist. Blackness.
The waves chase me. Wants to break me. Suffocate me. Torture me.
She calls out
'Leave it behind!'
Leave everything. Reject this pain. Search for truth. Search for peace.
The pain spreads. The mist grows thicker. Weighs me down.

Sarah Mannix

BARNET OF YESTERYEAR

Once these narrow streets had cobbled stones,
Horses hooves with harsh clattering tones
And fine carriages with ladies fair,
Busy people rushing here and there.

But all this was in the days gone by,
Horse-drawn coaches with their drivers high
Perched on small seats with a perfect view
To drive in chaos, to gallop through.

Cattle market sometimes in full swing,
Rock bottom prices on everything
And farmers flocked there with hope to buy,
Before soaring prices rose too high.

Barnet horse fair held then twice a year
Purchases were made by folks, far and near,
Such a happy time for people then,
Progress in life slow, but good for them.

Meetings with General William Booth
People listened, their anxieties soothed,
He was a great man of Hadley Wood,
Salvation Army founder doing good.

The trams that were never quite as fast
Small shops of character could not last,
Now Building Societies, banks with powers,
Shopping precinct with beautiful flowers.

Barnet College where students stand tall
Faces a church with one Norman wall.
2002, a conserved past,
Some listed buildings that last and last.

Although many changes have been made
Memories of yesteryear should not fade.

Irene Grahame

My Town

Stevenage new town, now not so new
It started off with just a few
Came from cities and from towns
To get a home, a magic sound

Some came from in-laws, shared rooms and a door
Others in furnished, all dingy and poor
To a house with three beds and a bathroom, oh boy
A garden with flowers for us to enjoy

Then like Alice, the town it just grew
Gathering us in, me, you and you
Some did not stay, but many more lingered
The roads curling outward pointing like fingers

Sporting people can be found
Many at the football ground
Happy shouting, calls and jeers
Sometimes losing, maybe tears

Town centre, meeting place for all
Fountain splashing near the wall
Theatre parks and swimming pool too
A perfect place for maybe you

Joyce Alderman

KEEPER OF THOUGHTS

Cloaked in sable night,
bathed in desert light.
Like a jewelled bauble
sparkling in the inky blue,
iridescent, peacock-tailed.
I am the sorcerer's sphere -
fire and ice in equal measure,
spewing and glaciered.
A snowflake in the eye of the storm.
A desiccated bed of rivers red.
All granite rock and velvet moss,
baptised in icicled waters
newly sprung and turquoise.
I am a silver-braided tendril,
infinite seeker of knowledge,
architect of webs,
keeper of thoughts.
I am radiant and I am eclipsed.
I am sound and I am silence.
I float, bereft of youth,
ancient, wrinkled, weathered,
light as whispered breath on mountain air,
yet heavy as sorrow.
I am alone, my song unanswered.
I am the world.

Lynda Bullock

Creeping Sickness

Way beneath the grey, green waves
The Murray eel and tiny fish
He hides, they dart and flaunt their colours
A huge basking shark passes with silent swish

Deep sea divers bubble around
What do they find now 'neath waters deep?
In this place, where delicate corals were found
Once an aura of colour now a rotting reef

Man's non appreciation of the beauty
That was given for man's delight
Now sewage and oil pollute the waves
Gone the vibrant colours, now a greyish white

How much longer will the bright fish small
And the shrinking species that we know
Survive? Soon there will be none left at all
Will this destruction ever stop and end this woe?

We hear of tumours on the turtles
Seals dying and going blind
Of dolphins caught in fishing nets
Treated as nothing, man is so unkind

The sadness in my heart
As this poem does unfurl
Is eased a little when I read
Of God's promise for a kind and bright new world.

J Howling Smith

The Downs And Around

Newly-cleaned tower
standing for all to see
on top of its small hill.

The lion
Now in his white summer coat
proudly pacing the downs,
overlooking the tower
surrounded by the flat land.

High above
looking down on both,
gliders effortlessly find the thermals
twisting and turning with the only sound,
a quiet thrumming
as they pass overhead.
Not enough to startle the deer
moving through the forest.

People outside the cafe
by the car park,
watch and look,
seeing the tower
and the gliders
but not the lion,
not from this ridge.
Some bring kites to fly,
vying with the hang-gliders
daringly dangling from a wing.

Gradually the hills slumber,
quiet darkness for the night creatures
scurrying their well-worn paths
unseen by human eye.
Peace.

Patricia Bull

Lessons Not Learned

The food tastes like sand
I know the routine,
I've been here before
Sleepless nights - every meal such a chore

But this time is worse
Or that's how it felt
I'd been broken through kindness
Not the fear of a belt

I've loved and I've needed
Was I going insane?
How could I fall for the
Same stupid game
    The rules may be different
    But the end, still the same

You say you're confused
All I feel is used
Out of the frying pan, into the fire?
God, I wish I'd left you stuck in that mire

They say anger is good
It releases the soul
But all it leaves me
Is a dirty great hole

You know I adore you
You're all I could ask
But instead I just feel
Like you've set me a task

So I've written out my pain
And expelled all the hate
Now all I can do
Is sit here and wait.

Rebecca Lee

Things Of Life

Most beautiful things of life are free
The hooting of an owl, the buzzing of the bee
The smell of a freshly new mown lawn
Crying of an infant, just been born
Crickets chirping across the fields
Flowers and herbs - their aroma yields
Holding your grandchild's tiny hand
Running barefoot across the sand
Sunset on a summer's eve
Waves crashing on a coral reef
Footprints in pure white snow
All these things are free we know
Appreciate them while we can
They can easily be taken away - by man

Christine Hardemon

AUTUMN

Autumn arrives and the leaves start to fall
And the hours of daylight are growing small
As sunlight fades and nights grow cold
The joys of spring are put on hold

The hedgehog finds a cosy den
To sleep all winter through and then
Wake up in the early spring
When snowdrops bloom and birds start to sing

Squirrels in winter search around
For nuts they've buried in the ground
Their food for the cold winter days
And when sated retire back to their drays

The birds find it hard going too
For flies and berries are but few
And worms are deep in the frozen ground
Out of reach and safe and sound

I think the swallows have got it right
When autumn comes they take to flight
To warmer climates they do go
And leave with the ice and snow

D W Mynott

The Empty Nest

My children have all upped and gone
The nest they've truly flown
No noise, no mess, no endless chores
The house is now my own

No more endless phone calls and
Friends knocking at the door
No more constant thumping of
Their music through the floor

No more messy bedrooms where
The beds are never made
No more lending fivers that
Somehow were not repaid

No more frantic swotting for
An unexpected test
No more soothing sounds of
'You can only do your best'

No more anxious waiting when
The hour is very late
No more broken hearts when
Young love turns to childish hate

So here I am, post children
With time at last for me
A pile of books for me to read
Friends joining me for tea

Why then, when I'm so happy
Why then, when I'm so glad
Do I still find from time to time
I really feel quite sad?

Christine Short

DEAR LORD

Thank you Lord for another day
It's time for bed and time to pray,
First I kneel and pray to you
Thanking you Lord, in all that you do.
Peace on earth is what we need,
Crops grow well so we may feed,
As you look down from Heaven above,
I feel your warmth and I feel your love.
As I grow old I still smile and grin,
Knowing you keep me from sin,
When I'm in pain I close my eyes
And lift my head towards the skies
And know my Lord you ease the pain
And stop it coming back again.
I prayed to you for your support
In World War II in which I fought.
My prayers were answered I send my love
And hope there's a place in Heaven above
Goodnight oh Lord, now I must sleep
And dream of you, as I count my sheep.

L Newcombe

St Valentine's Day

When I was young and still at school
And fancied a certain boy
I used to wait for Valentine's Day
With a heart so full of joy
I'd watch out for the postman
Who was always happy and gay
Whistling cheerfully down the road
At the same time every day
As the letters shuffled through the door
I'd watch them all with glee
But they were always for my sisters
And never one for me
My friends at school would get them
And wonder at their source
Many had six or seven
They made some up of course
Every year I hoped and prayed
That a Valentine card would come
But I never-ever got one
Not even sent by Mum
I wrote a lot of poems
For my friends to send their beaux
But I had ginger hair and freckles
And no boy fancied those
Then at the grand old age of 18
I found myself engaged
And lo and behold a Valentine came
I was happy but amazed
It was full of hearts and flowers

And so beautiful to see
After all those disappointing years
A Valentine just for me
I couldn't tell my schoolfriends
As my high school days had passed
Although I'd waited 18 years
I had got a card at last.

Anne D Tarbox

TWO PEOPLE

Just two people who long ago took care of me,
Two people who gave me all they could
Through everything they were there
I loved them dearly
Though as a child I did not understand all that they did
Through love alone
They loved me unconditionally asked for nothing in return
We're always there to guide and lend a helping hand
If I fell they picked me up
If I cried they dried my tears
If I was lost they found me
Anything I didn't understand, they tried to explain
They never questioned when I occasionally went wrong
Just guided me back to the right path
I tried to listen to their advice but didn't always understand,
Some times questioned what they said
But now I know they were mostly right
And what they did they did for me
They went through those very important years with me
And now that I'm grown and on my own
I do have one regret, that I never told them how I felt
And that my childhood was the happiest time of my life,
So I dedicate this poem to them with all my love,
For always being there
Just two people, my mum and dad.

Hazel Webb